TANDEM SIT-ON-TOP KAYAKING

By Tom Holtey

With Illustrations by Mike Altman

GEO ODYSSEY
PUBLICATIONS
PO Box 25441
Rochester, NY 14265

TANDEM SIT-ON-TOP KAYAKING
©Copyright 2000, by Tom Holtey
All rights reserved

First Edition / First Printing 2000

Published by GeoOdyssey Publications 2000
Printed in the United States of America

Heritage Cover photo by Daniel Forster
Cobra Tandem photo by Doug Peebles

Book Design by Athena Holtey

Illustrations by Mike Altman
©Copyright 2000 All rights reserved

About the Author

From his youth on the Charles River, Tom Holtey has accumulated nineteen years experience in the paddle sports industry with a foundation in canoeing and traditional sea kayaking. He has been involved in the sit-on-top field for the past ten years pioneering this new branch of the sport.

Trained and practiced in wilderness trip planning - from the White Mountains of New Hampshire and Maine to the tropical coastlines of the Hawaiian Islands - Tom, an alumni of the National Outdoor Leadership School or N.O.L.S., has lead and taught the novice adventurer under many varied conditions.

It was while teaching courses in sit-on-top kayaking at the University of Hawaii that much of his writing efforts began to take form. During this time, he managed a kayak retail store in Honolulu and worked with members of the local kayak club, Hui Wa'a Kaukahi, where many developments in the sport have been made.

In the fall of 1999 Tom and his wife Athena founded Sit-on-topKayaking.com, an online magazine and information exchange for open cockpit kayakers. Together they travel to kayak symposia throughout the country to promote sit-on-top kayaking and to educate the pioneers of this popular, fast evolving sport.

Acknowledgements

I would like to take this opportunity to thank the people who have helped me out along the way, including those who assisted with our first book: "Sit-on-top-top Kayaking, A Beginner's Guide."

*My wife **Athena** who has made it all possible.*

***Cam Holtey, Audrey Sutherland, Jim Brann, Dorothea Thornton-Mallon and Margaret McNab** for their help with editing.*

***Doug Peebles** for his photographic contributions.*

***Mike Altman** for his fantastic drawings.*

***Gary Budlong & John Enomoto** at Go Bananas for introducing me to sit-on-tops.*

***The folks at Hui Wa'a Kaukahi** for providing a fertile testing ground for sit-on-top development.*

***Steve Schneider,** and the many people in the paddlesports industry who have endorsed our efforts.*

*And finally to my **Mom** and **Dad** who have supported me in all my endeavors.*

There are still many others, not listed here, that have my fond gratitude for their kind fellowship during my voyages in life. You know who you are.

Sincerely,
Thomas O. Holtey Jr.

Table of Contents

About the Author 3
Acknowledgements 5
Introduction 11

Chapter 1 Why A Tandem?

Why a Tandem? 15

Chapter 2 Types of Tandem Kayaks

Play and Touring Tandems 19
Wave Skis 19
Surf Skis 21
Inflatable Kayaks 21

Chapter 3 Parts of a Tandem Kayak

Some Basics 23
A Closer Look 23
The Tandem Sit-on-top Kayak 24

Chapter 4 Accessories

The Kayak Paddle 27
The Life Jacket 28
Kayaking Apparel 28

Chapter 5 Who Sits Where?

Who Sits Where? 31

Chapter 6 Working As A Team

Working As A Team 33

Chapter 7 Launching and Landing

Launching From The Shore 35
Launching In Surf...35
Shallow Water Entry 36
Landing On Shore...38
The Surf Zone 38
Launching From A Dock................................39
Landing At A Dock 39

Chapter 8 Deep Water Re-entry

Deep Water Re-entry.....................................41

Chapter 9 Paddle Strokes

Finding Your Grip Zone.................................45
The Forward Stroke 45
A Note About Feathered Paddling 47
The Backstroke And Stopping 48
The Rudder Stroke 48
The Sweep Stroke..49
Bracing 51
Hula Hips...52
The Draw Stroke 52

Chapter 10 Important Seamanship Skills

Paddling In Wind...55
Tides 55
Rivers..56

Chapter 10 Important Seamanship Skills (con't.)

Paddling In Waves 56
Dealing With Currents And Wind 57

Chapter 11 Transporting Your Tandem

Foam Racks 59
Roof Racks 60
Car topping your kayak 60
Using Wheels 62

Chapter 12 Activities With Your Tandem

Fishing 65
Diving and Snorkeling 66
Camping With Your Tandem 67

Chapter 13 The Right Tandem For You

The Right Tandem for You 69

Chapter 14 Kayak Safety

Kayak Safety 71

Appendix

Safe Kayaking Check List 75
Glossary 77
Index 81
Resources 87
ORDER FORM 88

Table of Charts & Checklists 10
Table of Diagrams 10

Charts and Checklist

Types of Tandem Sit-on-tops 20
The Tandem Sit-on-top Kayak (Parts) 24
Kayak & Personal Gear Check List 29
Safe Kayaking Check List 75

Diagrams

Shallow Water Entry
    Step One: 36
    Step Two: 36
    Step Three 37
    Step Four: 37
Launching from a Dock 39
Deep Water Re-entry
    Step One 41
    Step Two 41
    Step Three 42
    Step Four 42
    Step Five 42
Forward Stroke
    (Front View) 46
Forward Stroke
    (Side View) 47
Reverse or Back Stroke 48
Rudder Stroke 49
Sweep Stroke
    (Front View) 49
    (Side View) 50
    (Pivoting Turn) 50

Bracing 51
The Draw Stroke 53
Car topping your kayak 61-62

Introduction

The topic of this book is to address the needs of tandem sit-on-top kayakers. It covers the basic skills necessary to have fun kayaking, safely, in the moderate conditions that average tandem kayakers might encounter.

If you are a solo sit-on-top kayaker, you should read the first book in this series: "Sit-on-top Kayaking, A Beginner's Guide." Both books are written to stand alone as beginning instruction to get you out on the water. Each book, however, does contain some unique information of interest to anyone taking up the sport.

Sit-on-top kayaks are more popular than ever before. This latest form of kayak is also called "open-cockpit," "wash-deck" and "open-top." Their introduction to the paddlesports world has brought the sport to many people who could not or would not paddle a sit-in-side kayak. By choosing these self-bailing models this new breed of paddler avoids the need to learn Eskimo rolling; can paddle free of a spray skirt; and is accomplishing the same goals with the same performance characteristics as traditional kayaks - in some cases surpassing the achievements of decked kayakers and their craft.

The primary reasons people are turning to open-cockpit kayaks are safety, convenience, and comfort.

Open-top kayaks *are* safer than their decked counterparts. Exposure to cold water is the number one hazard for kayakers, but a sit-on-top paddler can get back onto their kayak from deep water in seconds.

Wash-deck kayaks are also easy to learn and use. Because they are self-bailing there is no need to learn Eskimo rolling. It is a good skill to have, but few learn it well enough to use in true survival situations. Because they are "open" getting in and out of your kayak is a much simpler task. The use of paddle floats for deep-water reentry is almost unheard of.

Sit-on-tops are more comfortable. Paddlers do not have to squeeze into a hole in their boat. Quite a few people are more at ease sitting "on top" rather than "down in." Because open-top paddlers do not use spray skirts they can have a tall backrest for extra support and comfort. They can even put their feet up and relax, or sit sidesaddle and dangle them in the water.

While this book does not cover the use of sit-in-side kayaks many of the principles described in it apply also to that form of craft. If you are looking for a thorough study of technical information on seamanship, navigation, equipment, whitewater technique, and skills, there are many excellent books out there for you to choose from. Currently, most of them are from a "sit-inside" perspective, but still filled with lots of valuable information to enrich your skills as you continue to pursue this exciting sport.

Tandem Sit-on-top Kayaking

Why a Tandem?

With the addition of sit-on-top tandem kayaks to the paddlesports fleet one can paddle a kayak that is unswampable, and requires no eskimo rolling or bailing. An open cockpit tandem kayak is at the cutting edge of the paddling world.

Years ago it was the canoe that introduced most of us to paddlesports. This original North American two-person paddle craft was designed for carrying loads on our many waterways. However the high sides catch wind. The high seats decrease stability and the deckless construction insures the craft will swamp after a capsize.

Over time paddlers favored kayaks over canoes not only because of their speed and sleekness, their sea worthiness in wind, waves, and white water rivers, but also for the feeling of independence that paddling a solo boat offers. This sit-*inside* or decked kayak, also a North American paddle craft, was designed to carry a solo hunter into the field and bring back game, often by towing.

A lower seat added stability and allowed for a skinny sleek hull. A lower profile close to the water decreased the wind's push on the kayak. Two and even three-person kayaks were developed, akin to the multi person Bidarkas of the Pacific Northwest. The deck of the kayak and the spray skirt eliminated the problem of capsizing, but knowing how to Eskimo roll became vital.

In just the past few decades inovative people, largely from Australia and California, took paddling to its next evolution creating the "sit-on-top" solo kayak. In more recent years its popularity has spread not only to the lands of the original canoes and kayaks, but throughout the world.

This trend toward the solo kayak left a void in the assembly of small craft that had once been filled by the canoe; so it seems only natural that tandem sit-on-top kayaks are the fastest growing branch of this new evolution of the sport. This self-bailing boat requires no eskimo rolling or spray skirt. A sealed compartment below deck provides buoyancy even after a capsize. The solo versions were the first of this new development to emerge and now all the major kayak companies are producing both tandem and solo sit-on-top kayaks.

Oddly enough this has brought the technology of paddling full circle to the first human who carved a shallow cockpit in a log to carry a family and their possessions across the water.

The tandem is allowing us to regain the teamwork and togetherness that a canoe once provided. With the sit-on-top tandem we can have the best of both worlds in a two-person craft that will handle strong winds, rough water, and ocean conditions safely.

When kayaking with solo boats, paddlers become separated by distance and communication is difficult. This may be fine for those with an independent personality, but others may want a sense of teamwork and togetherness.

Some paddling partners do not want to be in separate boats for a variety of good reasons. Tandem kayakers can talk to each other with ease and work together as a team. Being close and sharing the experience is one of the best motives for using a two-person craft.

Most notably, families with children will be keen to take advantage of tandem kayaks which have multiple seats. This allows adults to keep the kids together and eliminates straying.

A two-seater also makes it possible for a novice kayaker to join an experienced paddler in the enjoyment of a water environment that may be beyond their ability as a solo kayaker.

Whatever your reasons for choosing a tandem sit-on-top kayak and purchasing this book, I am sure that if you apply the principles taught here you will find tandem kayaking to be a fun and rewarding sport for you and your crew.

You will want to begin the development of your kayaking endevors with instruction. A book like this is a good place to start. It will provide some information to help you venture out onto the water with confidence and provide a reference for brushing up on your skills.

However, there is no better source of training than a qualified instructor in a class setting. Seek out kayak classes in your area. Take the class with your paddling partner. Most kayaking classes are for solo paddlers in sit-in-side kayaks. Don't be shy. Ask if you can paddle a sit-on-top kayak. If not, then take the class anyway. Almost all the information in the course will be of use. You will each learn faster if you paddle your own solo boat, but you should have the opportunity to paddle a double kayak in the lesson program.

I hope you will also take the opportunity to visit our website and others. Participate in the many paddlesports forums on the internet or just read through them, learning from others who have been where you are going.

And, finally, establish a good relationship with your local kayak shop. They will prove to be the best source for information about your area and the conditions you will be paddling in.

Types of Tandem Kayaks

From Specialized to Multiuse

There are several forms that tandem open cockpit kayaks come in. You will find them built for a variety of uses such as touring, play, scuba, wave riding, and racing. Kayaks that do one job very well often do other jobs poorly. Kayaks that do many jobs usually will not excel at all the tasks that they try to accommodate. Carefully consider what kind of kayaker you and your partners are. Select a kayak that is appropriate for you needs.

Play and Touring Tandems

The most common kayaks are the general purpose play and touring kayaks. These boats are designed for utility and fun. Stability and ease of use are the primary characteristics. This makes them excellent for family outings, fishing, play, surfing, camping, scuba diving, and snorkeling. Kayaks in this category range from 12 to 16 feet long. Most are made of tough plastic. There is often a place to store cargo such as coolers and camping, diving or fishing gear. Kids can also ride in these cargo areas. Many tandems are also designed with a center seat to accommodate a solo paddler. This allows the kayak to do double duty of solo and tandem paddling.

Shorter, wider tandems are very suitable to day trips, surfing and play. These fun-loving craft are often very stable and a little slower. Some of these boats have a considerable amount of cargo space and could be appropriate for camping trips and light scuba adventures.

Longer, slimmer tandems will paddle along at a faster, easier pace, making them a good choice for touring. Many of these kayaks also have good cargo space and do very well on camping trips that involve longer distances. They are often more suited to scuba adventures and other activities that require a lot of gear.

Wave Skis

There are a limited number of tandem wave skis available. A wave ski is a cross between a surfboard and a kayak. Most are

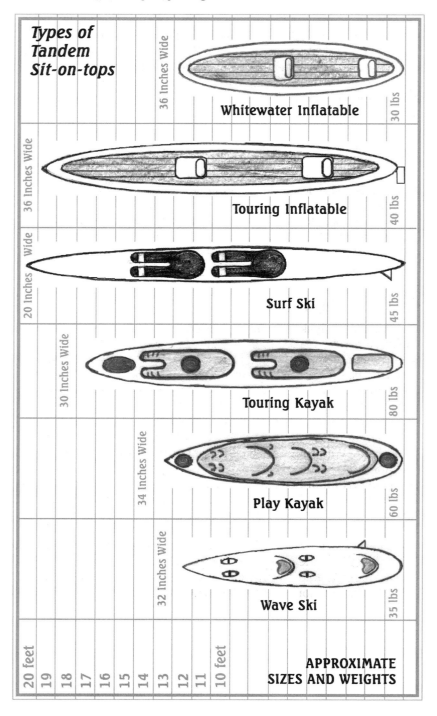

Types of Tandem Sit-on-tops

36 Inches Wide

Whitewater Inflatable — 30 lbs

36 Inches Wide

Touring Inflatable — 40 lbs

20 Inches Wide

Surf Ski — 45 lbs

30 Inches Wide

Touring Kayak — 80 lbs

34 Inches Wide

Play Kayak — 60 lbs

32 Inches Wide

Wave Ski — 35 lbs

20 feet 19 18 17 16 15 14 13 12 11 10 feet

APPROXIMATE SIZES AND WEIGHTS

designed for a solo rider. If you look hard enough you will find a two-person model. They have flat bottoms with fins that allow them to hydroplane on an ocean wave face for an exhilarating ride.

Almost all wave skis are made of composite materials. If you are looking for a kayak strictly for tandem surfing then look for one of these.

Surf Skis

You don't have to race competitively to enjoy a tandem surf ski. A surf ski is a very long, skinny and fast open cockpit kayak. They are built for speed, and are not as stable as touring kayaks. Most surf skis are for solo racing, but there are a few models built for tandem racing. All are made of composite materials. If you are looking for speed or have a competitive spirit then a surf ski is for you.

Inflatable Kayaks

Inflatable kayaks are usually built for two people. Many have seats that can be placed in the center for solo paddling. This category can be diverse. Most inflatables are designed for white water rivers. These are sometimes called "rubber ducks." You will see more inflatable, "soft shell," sit-on-tops on white-water rivers than "hard shell" sit-on-tops. For tandem river running an inflatable is currently your only choice in an open-deck boat.

There are touring models that are better suited for flat water. Some come with rudders to hold your course in open water. Inflatables are made of vinyl, synthetic or natural rubber. You inflate them with a foot or hand operated air pump. They are not as fragile as they may seem. Many are quite strong, but that doesn't mean that you can be careless with them. Inflatables are meant to store and transport conveniently; this is there primary function. Performance takes a back seat to transportability. Apartment dwellers and travelers are the most common users of this style of craft. Choose an inflatable if you want to take a kayak on a bus or a plane, or if you want to store it under your bed or in a closet.

Parts of a Tandem Kayak

You will want to familiarize your self with the parts and accessories of your kayak. The kayak will come with some preinstalled features but you will have to add some equipment to make the outfit complete.

Some Basics

The front of the kayak is called the *bow*. The back of the kayak is called the *stern*. The top of the kayak is the *deck* and the bottom is called the *hull*. The place where the people sit is called the *cockpit(s)* and the edge of the boat where the cockpit meets the hull is the *gunwale*. There is a *seat* for your rear end and places for your feet called the *footwells*.

A Closer Look

Most tandem kayaks come with *handles* bow and stern. These allow for two people to carry the kayak. They can also be used to attach bowlines, leashes, towlines, and anchor ropes.

A *drain plug* may be installed to let out water that has leaked in to the hull. It would be located near the bow or stern. To empty this water, open the plug and turn your boat over, while on the land, and let the water drain out. Lately, *ropes* or *shock cords* have come preinstalled to the deck in various configurations. These are for handholds or for the attachment of cargo.

Deck lines, backrest, and many other accessories are mounted to the deck using *strap eyes*. These are loops that are riveted or screwed in place.

The Tandem Sit-on-top Kayak

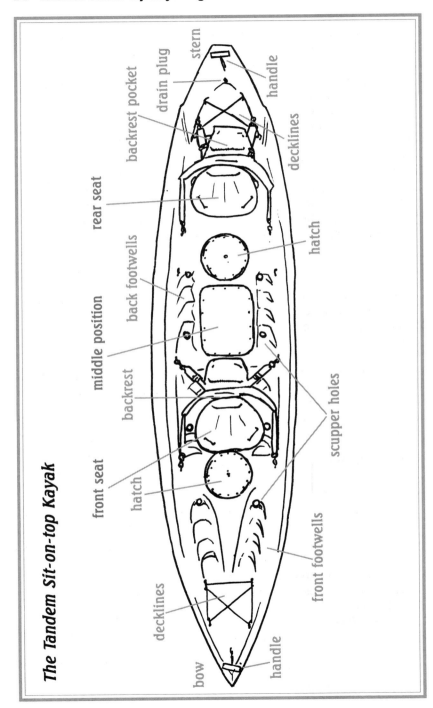

stern

drain plug

handle

backrest pocket

decklines

rear seat

hatch

back footwells

hatch

middle position

backrest

scupper holes

front seat

hatch

front footwells

decklines

bow

handle

Kayaks also utilize **cargo straps** to secure gear in the external storage area. If not preinstalled, your kayak can be customized with these amenities to fit your needs.

Scupper holes are the drains from the seating areas back into the sea. This is what makes the kayak self-bailing. When water splashes into the cockpit it drains, by gravity, into the scuppers in the seat and or foot wells. This water flows down through tubes in the hull and out the bottom of the boat back into the body of water you are paddling in. The larger the scupper holes, or the more scupper holes, the faster the kayak will drain. Some boats have one big hole and others have many small holes. While the scuppers are not meant to let water in the cockpit a small amount can flow up the tube and get the rider damp. It is possible to cork these holes. Some sit-on-top kayaks come with the corks or they can be obtained as an accessory. It is possible to produce your own corks from recycled material, like foam rubber and natural cork.

Storage hatches come in many styles and sizes. This allows the users of the kayak to store items below deck and out of the way. Some hatches have lids that screw in like the lid of a jar. Other hatches open and close with knobs; some secure with straps and buckles.

It will not be completely dry in the hull of your kayak. If you want something to remain dry, store it in a **waterproof bag** or case. A small amount of water in the hull is not a problem but a lot of water in the hull could indicate a leak.

A **rudder** may be an option for your kayak. This is a blade that is mounted on the stern, at the water line, and pivots right or left to

 aid in turning your kayak. The rudder blade is connected to foot pedals in the cockpit by cables. This allows the rear paddler and, in some cases, the front paddler, to steer the kayak with their feet. Push on the left to go left and push on the right to go right. You can always steer with your paddle, and you will be a better paddler for it. However, a rudder can be very helpful in conditions when the wind and the waves come from behind or from the side.

A **bowline** can be fastened to the front handle. This multi purpose rope can be used for tying your kayak to a buoy on the water, a tree at the beach, or for towing another kayak.

A *paddle leash* is a device that attaches the paddle to the kayak. It is usually a coil cord that has a Velcro closure for the paddle shaft and fastens to the deck or bowline. Some paddle leashes are constructed of shock cord, often inserted into a tubular webbing 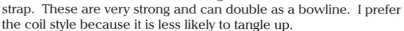 strap. These are very strong and can double as a bowline. I prefer the coil style because it is less likely to tangle up.

A *lifeline* is a rope that attaches to your kayak and has a large loop to put your head and one arm through. The loop is tied so that it can not tighten and is large enough to put on and take off easily. The lifeline is used to keep the kayak from blowing away from you after a capsize in windy conditions. No one can swim fast enough to catch a drifting kayak in high winds. Some paddlers have used a surf board leash for the same purpose, but hazards could result from using a lifeline with your kayak in the surf zone.

The *backrest* is largely a comfort device. Without a backrest you may be uncomfortable due to the lack of support. On a very short trip this may be ok, but on a long trip you will want one. While it is not always necessary to have backrests for children, it can help keep them in place on the kayak and afford them the same perceived status of others who do have them. The front straps of the backrest attach to the kayak on each side of the cockpit near the knees. The back straps attach just behind the seat: two straps in front and two straps behind.

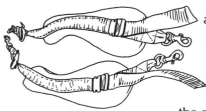

Knee straps are performance accessories that help the paddlers maintain control of the tilt and lean of the kayak. Knee straps are particularly useful in rough water and wave surfing. Each strap is fastened to the front near the ankles and to the rear near the hips on the same side. You will need to adjust the backrest and the knee straps to fit your shape and size. Customizing the attachment locations can also increase comfort and performance.

Accessories

PADDLES, LIFE VESTS & APPAREL

The Kayak Paddle

The paddle is your primary tool used to make the kayak move. It consists of a shaft with a paddle blade at each end. They come in a variety of sizes, shapes and styles.

Longer paddles are for large people and/or wide kayaks. Shorter paddles are for small people and/or narrow kayaks.

Children should have paddles that are long enough for them to reach the water comfortably, and to grow into.

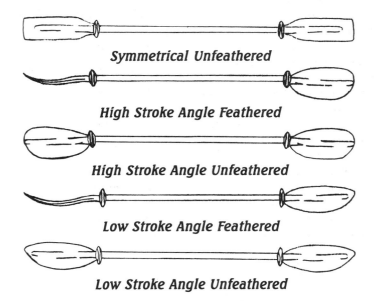

Symmetrical Unfeathered

High Stroke Angle Feathered

High Stroke Angle Unfeathered

Low Stroke Angle Feathered

Low Stroke Angle Unfeathered

Blade shapes will determine the paddle's performance.

➢ **Shorter, wider, symmetrical blades** are for paddlers who use a high stroke angle, with the shaft held almost vertically. This type of paddle is good for power and rough water play.

➢ A **longer asymmetrical blade** is for a low stroke angle, with the shaft held almost horizontal. This type of paddle is good for long distance and a relaxed style.

A quick easy way to fit your paddle is to hold it up like a staff and touch the blade tip with your fingers. You should be able to just reach the top with your arm extended. A knowledgeable instructor or kayak salesperson can help you get the right fit.

The Life Jacket

The life vest, or **Personal Floatation Device (PFD)**, is your most important piece of equipment. It should fit comfortably but snug. Try on many different P.F.D.s before choosing one as your own.

Look for a vest with a short waistline and large armholes. To make sure it will fit and be comfortable do these trials:

➤ Sit in a kayak or on the floor with the life vest on to make sure the vest will not ride up around your neck.

➤ Swing your arms around windmill style to check for full freedom of motion.

➤ Then try the vest in the water for a final test. Use the adjustment straps to make a snug fit. It should float you comfortably without riding up, slipping off, or rolling you face down.

Children's life vests are available in several sizes. Make sure that the vest that you are using for your kids is the right size for their weight range.

This information is printed on a label that is sewn into the vest. Sometimes the print is very small. You may want to write the weight limit on the vest with a marker. Never compromise safety by using the wrong size vest. If you have kids, get a selection of children's vests in assorted sizes. Then you will be able to fit all your children and their friends. They are worth the investment.

Kayaking Apparel

Clothing that is appropriate to the water environment is essential. Always dress as if you are going to swim in the water. There is always a possibility that any kind of boat can capsize. Wearing protective apparel is like putting your seat belt on in the car; you do it every day but you do not have an accident every day.

Quick drying nylon pants and a shirt are good for warm water and fair weather. A combination of polyester fleece and a splash

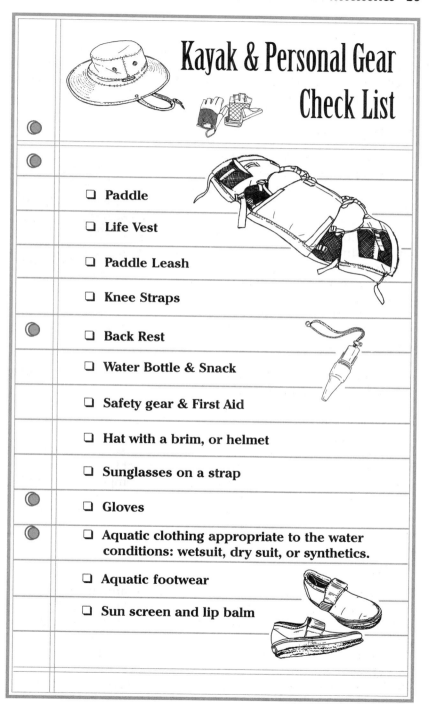

Kayak & Personal Gear Check List

- ❑ Paddle
- ❑ Life Vest
- ❑ Paddle Leash
- ❑ Knee Straps
- ❑ Back Rest
- ❑ Water Bottle & Snack
- ❑ Safety gear & First Aid
- ❑ Hat with a brim, or helmet
- ❑ Sunglasses on a strap
- ❑ Gloves
- ❑ Aquatic clothing appropriate to the water conditions: wetsuit, dry suit, or synthetics.
- ❑ Aquatic footwear
- ❑ Sun screen and lip balm

proof shell is sufficient for moderate conditions.

Cold water robs the body of heat. This can debilitate, if not kill a person. The longer you are in the water or the colder the water is the greater the risk of hypothermia. Know the temperature of the waters you paddle in and dress appropriately.

Wet suits are for cold water and paddling far from shore. A dry suit (with an insulation layer underneath) will provide you the best protection from hypothermia. Add to your outfit: a wide brimmed hat (neoprene hood for cold water), gloves (pogies for cold water), and neoprene boots.

Find out what kind of clothing is recommended and used in your area. Have an assortment of aquatic apparel that is appropriate for all the seasons and conditions that you paddle in.

Children also need to wear such protective clothing. It will be difficult to find all you need in their size, but if you look hard you may find wet suits and shoes in kids sizes. Don't push your luck by being unprepared.

Who Sits Where? 5

The big question in tandem kayaking is: Who Sits Where?

There are many ways to address this question. Seating arrangements can be made based on experience, weight, preference, practicality, and maintaining harmony among the crew.

The primary reason for someone to sit in the rear is experience. The person in the back seat steers the kayak. A paddler with more experience will be better able to direct the kayak, making course decisions based on previous paddling situations. How does one get this kind of knowledge? By sitting in the back seat and steering the kayak of course! On fair weather days it is advisable to let inexperienced paddlers take the steering seat and learn the skills that will enable them to guide the boat wisely.

Sometimes the weight of the paddlers will determine who sits in each seat. A kayak is best loaded evenly, or if necessary, a bit more weight in the rear. Some tandem sit-on-tops can not handle the weight of a large person in the front seat. A kayak will handle best if bow is loaded lighter than stern, unless paddling into very strong winds or currents where more weight in the bow is better. So it is safe to say when in doubt put the larger person in the back and the smaller person in the front.

Other reasons to choose front or rear seats are as follows: A person who is handling a fishing pole may want to sit in the bow so the stern paddler, who will have better control of the kayak, can direct the boat. The same is true for bird watching with binoculars.

Some people just have to be the "captain" (sits in the rear), others just want to be the "crew" (sits in the bow). It may also be a matter of personal preference. If possible, sit where you like it best.

If you must paddle a two-person kayak, solo you will want to sit in the middle seat, if it has one, or the back seat. You will have the best control of your boat by sitting in the middle, good control if you sit in the rear, and poor control if you are in the front seat. You can put a load, such as a cooler or a dog, in the front seat to balance the boat.

When paddling with children you will want to seat them depending on certain circumstances. Very small children are best seated in the lap of an adult. Larger children ride best in their own seats or a suitable storage well on the deck.

In a three-seat kayak, with a party of two adults and one child, put the adults in the front and back seats and the child in the middle. This allows for either adult to attend to the child. If you are one adult and two children then you may put the kids in the front and back seats while you control the boat from the center seat. Putting the children in the bow and mid seats while you sit in the rear helps trim the weight in the kayak properly. Some times you can put two small children in the same seat. Always bear in mind the weight capacity of the kayak. Also the more wiggling bodies you put on board the greater your chances of a capsize. The weight of kids is not just cargo but a "dynamic cargo" that moves around and leans over the side unpredictably.

You must be prepared to apply all these principles to your seating choices. There are no black and white rules of seating. You must experiment and be flexible with the possibilities depending on the conditions and the passengers involved.

Working as a Team

Working together as a team is an important part of tandem kayaking. Following the procedures outlined in this book, being patient with your partner, and communicating are the keys to a successful and enjoyable paddling experience.

The ability to talk to one another is a reason that many choose a tandem kayak. However there is a problem with this notion that has a very simple solution. The front rider is facing away from the rear. The bow paddle's mouth and ears are pointing forward. This makes it difficult for the person in the stern to hear what the bow rider says and be heard when the rear rider is speaking. The solution is for the bow paddler to turn their head to the side when speaking and when they want to hear the back person. This points one ear directly to the stern paddler and directs at least half of their voice rearward.

You and your partner need to communicate about how you intend to handle the boat. The bow paddler is the eyes of the kayak and they need to direct the stern paddler on how to steer the kayak around obstacles that can not seen by the stern paddler. The front person blocks the view of the rear person. When it comes to making general decisions about where to go and what course to follow I suggest that you be democratic. This will eliminate "Captain Bligh syndrome" and the resulting mutiny and unhappiness that result. You are a team, make compromises as necessary.

Until you and your partner can anticipate each other's moves and goals it will be wise to state your intentions to each other to avoid confusion. Don't be shy. Count out strokes or sing "row, row, your boat" to keep the paddling rhythm. Tell your partner what you wish to do as points of interest present themselves. Indicate to your partner what strokes you want to do to accomplish certain maneuvers.

Launching and Landing

Launching from the Shore

When the time comes to launch your two-person kayak you should follow this procedure. Diagrams demonstrating these techniques are illustrated on the the following two pages.

➤ Put on your life vests and check your kayak and gear to insure that all is in order.
➤ Bring the kayak into shallow water, bow first, so that the person who will be in the front seat is in water about knee deep. Make sure that the hull is not going to be grounded when the kayak is loaded with the riders.
➤ If you are the front person, place your paddle in the water on the opposite side of the kayak. The paddle won't get away because of the leash.
➤ Then put your hands on each side of the boat to steady it while you sit on the seat sidesaddle. The other person keeps the kayak from drifting.
➤ When you, the front rider, are stable, lift your legs into the foot wells and pick up your paddle.
➤ The rear rider pushes the kayak into water that is knee deep for him/her.

As the rear paddler you will get in using the same technique while the front person braces with their paddle if necessary.

If there are small children riding they will get in first while an adult holds the kayak steady in water shallow enough for the kid(s) to enter the boat.

Launching in Surf

In surf zone conditions you may require additional help from paddling partners or bystanders on the shore.

In this case, one or more people will hold the kayak steady while the riders mount the kayak as described above.

Then the people holding the boat will give it a mighty shove forward while the riders paddle vigorously until they have passes the surf zone. *(For more information on surf, see Chapter 10, "Important Seamanship skills.")*

Shallow Water Entry

Step One:

The front rider places a hand on each side of the kayak while the rear rider steadies the boat...

Step Two:

The front rider sits in the seat side-saddle with their legs overboard...

Step Three

The front rider places their feet into the footwells...

Step Four:

The Front rider braces, if necessary, while the rear rider enters the kayak using the same method...

Landing on Shore

Landing your tandem kayak is similar to the launch but in reverse. While you can plow your kayak onto the shore and step out onto the beach, you will find the following method easy and graceful:

> ➢ As the boat approaches the shore the front rider will dismount by putting their feet over-board on one side into knee-deep water and stand up.
> ➢ Then with the paddle in one hand, pull the kayak shoreward by the bow handle. Pause to let the rear rider off in knee deep water.
> ➢ Now, pull the craft together, up the beach to the high water mark. If there are children on board an adult should hold the boat in shallow water while they get out.

The Surf Zone

Surf zone landings are often a crash, even for the most experienced, but timing and practice can help you pull them off smoothly.

Approach the beach carefully. Stay clear of swimmers and waders. As the boat nears the shore, the front paddler will hop out first, the rear paddler next, and then together pull the kayak out of the water quickly, as described above.

If the waves are pushing your kayak strongly to shore it may be necessary for the rear paddler to back-paddle a bit while the front rider dismounts. In very strong surf the rear paddler may even have to get off the kayak first in deeper water to act as a sea anchor by holding onto the rear handle of the kayak.

In this case, the front rider will get off in thigh deep water and pull the kayak shore ward. When the rear paddler can touch bottom, both will pull the kayak up the beach to the high water mark.

Your tandem will want to turn sideways in the surf and roll like a log to the beach. If you crash on your way to the landing; fear not. The waves will wash both riders and boat to the shore in most cases. Wade to shallow waters and approach your kayak cautiously. Kayaks in shallow surf pull and buck like obstinate mules. The waves push the kayak around forcefully. This can cause the kayak to strike you painfully in the shins, or worse. Anticipate the way the kayak will be pushed by the waves, grab it and pull it ashore quickly.

Launching from a Dock

To launch your tandem from a dock follow this proceedure:

➤ Have your paddling partner hold the kayak while it is floating next to the dock.

➤ You will place your paddle on the dock and across to the deck of the kayak just behind the seat, like a bridge.

➤ Sit on the dock with your feet in the footwells of the boat.

➤ With one hand on the paddle shaft over the dock and the other hand on the shaft over the deck, put your weight on the shaft and shift your butt onto the seat.

➤ Your paddling partner will do the same as you hold the dock from the cockpit of the kayak.

Landing at a Dock

To get back onto the dock you will use this procedure in reverse, as follows:

➤ Place your paddle behind you on the deck of your kayak and across to the dock.

➤ While your paddling partner holds the dock you put your weight on the shaft and lift your butt up onto the dock, seated with your feet still in the boat.

Then your partner will do the same while you hold the boat.

Deep Water Re-entry 8

Getting back on your kayak from deep water is one of the most important things that you need to know. The ability to get back on your kayak dependably and quickly can make a big difference, especially in a cold-water environment. Getting on your sit-on-top tandem is easy if you practice and follow these principles.

Step One

...reach for the far side...

If you have fallen off your boat chances are that your partner has also. First turn the boat right side up, if necessary. Then get on opposite sides of the kayak making sure that your paddle, attached by a leash, is clear from your side. One at a time reach for the far side of the boat, grabbing the gunwale, knee strap or backrest strap. Gripping with one hand on the close side and one on the far side is preferable.

Step Two

Pull yourself across the seat...

Pull yourself across the seat area with your arms and a forceful swimmer's kick with your legs. Allow the kayak to tilt a little making it easy to get aboard. Now you are lying across the kayak on your belly.

Step Three

Sit side-saddle

Roll over so your butt slides into the seat while your hands are on each side of the boat. Now you are sitting sidesaddle in the seat. Take a moment to gain stability and then put your feet into the foot wells.

Step Four

Place your feet into the foot wells...

Gather up your paddle and prepare to brace with your paddle as necessary. This can be done one at a time by having one person get on first while the other, in the water, holds the kayak steady. Then the second rider can get on board while the first braces with their paddle.

Step Five

Prepare to brace...

See the section on bracing in the strokes chapter. It is possible for both paddlers to reenter the kayak together but good timing and practice will be necessary. Practice in water over your head but not too far from shore. Do not venture out into deep-off shore waters until you have mastered this procedure and can do it easily every time.

If you are paddling with children, you must practice deep-water reentry with the kids. Make this practice into a game, it will be fun, and when it happens for real it will not be frightening.

Put the kids on the kayak in water that you can wade in but is deep to them. With the kids on board pretend that the water is rough. Children love to rock boats and pretend that they are in a storm at sea. Play up to their imagination. Introduce the idea that the "ship" may capsize and that they will have to swim.

Gently turn the kayak enough to spill the kids out. It is not necessary to turn the boat over; this could cause an unhappy bump on the head. They may want to turn the kayak over themselves, and that is ok as long as care is taken not to injure any one. Now let them climb back on board.

Some children will get on very easily, others will not. It will depend on their size and ability to grasp, pull, and kick. After some time with this you will be able to assess their ability and join in the fun. Kids love this kind of play and seem to enjoy it for hours, especially on a hot summer's day.

You and your children will be able to develop a routine procedure to reenter the kayak as a group, with adults and children getting on board at the optimal times.

Very small children will likely need to be lifted onto the kayak by an adult seated in the cockpit. Use you legs as a landing ramp while sitting sidesaddle with your feet in the water. An adult may want to get on board first to minimize tipping, assist the children, or brace as necessary. If there are two adults one may want to stay in the water to corral the youngsters. Larger children will be more like adults in their ability to climb on the kayak and brace with their paddles as others climb on.

Paddle Strokes 9

You will need to learn some basic maneuvers to make your kayak move and to control its direction. You accomplish this by using your primary tool, the paddle. Learning how to perform different paddle strokes to achieve these maneuvers is the subject of this chapter.

You will learn the *forward stroke* to move forward, the *backstroke* to stop and move backwards, the *sweep* and *rudder strokes* for turning, the *brace* for maintaining stability, and the *draw* for going sideways.

Practice them in open water not too far from shore. Try your turning strokes and draw strokes in combination with your forward and reverse strokes. Use buoys and other obstacles to maneuver around for practice. If any one is curious about your routine tell them you are practicing for a kayak ballet.

Finding Your Grip Zone

Grasp the shaft of your paddle with both hands, knuckles pointed forward. To find the proper grip zone place the center of the paddle shaft on the top of your head. Hold the paddle like a chin-up bar. Your hands should be directly above your elbows with your forearms straight up and down.

This is the recommended grip area; however, you might be more comfortable with your grip slightly toward the center. Everyone eventually develops their own paddling style, gleaning from the expert advice around them. Your hands are not glued to the paddle shaft and you can shift your grip as you feel the need to.

The Forward Stroke

You will be using the forward stroke more than any other stroke. It is what provides your power for getting around. The technique explained here is the same for the front and rear paddlers.

To do the forward stroke place your paddle blade in the water near your foot position. Using your lower hand as a fulcrum, push forward with the upper hand so that the shaft levers the blade in the water backward toward your hip. Do this alternately on the right and left sides with the right and left paddle blades to achieve forward momentum.

Push more with the upper arm and pull less with the lower arm. This will work the larger back and shoulder muscles, and relive the smaller arm muscles.

You can use your abdominal muscles as well by twisting a bit at the waist to face your paddle shaft as it angles right and left. Keep your paddle shaft low and parallel to the water for stability and ease

*Forward Stroke
(Front View)*

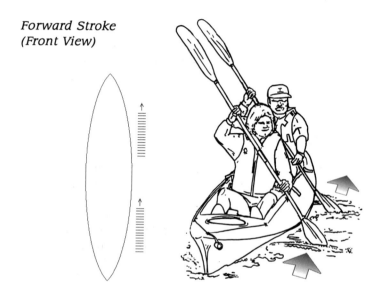

or, if you wish, at a high angle to the water for power and speed.

To work together as a team you will need to synchronize your paddle strokes. The bow and stern paddlers will place their blades in the water on the same side and stroke together. Not on opposite sides like a canoe.

Take a stroke on the right together and then a stroke on the left, right again, left again and so forth. There will be some paddle clashing while learning. Do not let that discourage you; it is normal.

To avoid smacking your paddles follow this simple principle:

➢ The front person sets the pace. It will be necessary for that person to set a steady and predictable rhythm.

➢ The back person will follow that pace. The stern paddler can see what the bow paddler is doing and has the ability to follow their lead.

Forward Stroke
(Side View)

The bow paddler can not see the stern paddler and so can not anticipate their moves. It may be helpful to count out left and right stokes aloud, or sing a song to help maintain a rhythm. Clashing paddles is not an opportunity to point blame. It is no one's fault, it just happens. As you practice together it will happen less and less.

A Note About Feathered Paddling

The beginning kayaker will often be mystified by the feathered paddle. The reason for the feathered paddle is wind resistance. The returning blade cuts through the air as the other blade pushes on the water. In a strong head wind this can save a lot of energy.

In most modern kayak paddles a center connector in the shaft allows it to be twisted to accommodate two or more angles.

The unfeathered paddle has blades that are parallel. Use of this type of paddle is very intuitive and requires no special technique. The feathered paddle, however, has blades that are as much as forty-five to ninety degrees offset. This requires a bit of know how to use.

The grip on your feathered paddle is firm, not too tight, with the right hand, and loose with the left hand (Left handed people can do oppositely.)

Your knuckles should line up with the centerline of the back of the right blade. The right wrist controls the angle of the blade. Hold your paddle out in front of you like the handle bar of a motorcycle. Turn the "accelerator" on by twisting your right wrist. Let the shaft turn freely in the left hand. Imagine glue in your right hand and grease in your left hand.

The shaft and blades will rotate. You are now controlling the angle of the blade.

Incorporate this into your forward stroke. Take a stroke with the right blade. Rotate the shaft to realign the left blade and take another stroke on the left, then rotate the shaft back and take a stroke in the right side.

Keep repeating this and you are paddling feathered.

The Backstroke and Stopping

When you need to stop you can put on the breaks by paddling backwards. The backstroke is the opposite of the forward stroke.

Place your paddle in the water by your hip and push forward to slow or stop the kayak. You can use the backside of the paddle blade. It does not have to be the powerface that pushes the water.

Reverse or Back Stroke

You must take stokes on each side, like the forward stroke, or you will turn in reverse. Take a back stoke on the right and then the left, alternating right and left strokes until you have slowed the kayak sufficiently or stopped.

Of course you will need to work together as a team by synchro-nizing your efforts. If you want to go in reverse just backpaddle. From a forward moving course, you can back paddle until you've slowed, stopped, and then begin to move in reverse. Or you can reverse from a dead stop. Apply the same team work principles that you would if you were using the forward stroke.

The Rudder Stroke

The rudder stroke is for making small course corrections while the kayak is in motion. The stern paddler is the only one to rudder the kayak. The bow paddler can only rudder the kayak if it is going in reverse.

If you are the back paddler, and you want to make a small course correction while moving forward, place your paddle blade in the water on the side of the boat that you want to turn toward. The

Rudder Stroke

blade is held at a slight angle to the direction of travel, just behind you. This creates drag on that side of the kayak and slows that side down.

You will lose some forward momentum and speed while doing this stroke. It is best to rudder very slightly at the end of each forward stroke over the course of several strokes until you are on your intended path.

If you make one big rudder stoke you will slow your kayak and get out of step with your partner. You can only use the rudder stroke if the kayak is moving. If you are moving backwards the bow paddler can deploy their paddle as a rudder by using the same technique placing the blade far forward and near the bow.

The Sweep Stroke

The sweep stroke is a powerful turning stroke that enables you to control the direction your kayak is pointing in.

The sweep is similar to the forward stroke, but instead of pulling your paddle in a strait line along the side of the boat, you

Sweep Stroke
(Front View)

sweep your paddle blade in a wide arc out away from the boat. This should look like a letter C from a top view.

The sweep stroke can be done in reverse, like the forward stroke, to have an opposite effect on the kayak.

Sweep Stroke
(Side View)

To make a wide turn both paddlers can sweep on the same side. Your kayak will turn to the opposite side that the stroke is performed on. This will make the kayak start to turn on a circular path, eventually describing a full circle in the water as the stoke is repeated on the same side. Very little momentum will be lost when using this stroke.

The rear paddler can use the paddle as a rudder while the front paddler performs a sweep on the opposite side. This will have a similar effect as both paddlers sweeping on the same side but will make for a much tighter turn, eventually describing a smaller circle. Some momentum will be lost because the rudder stroke slows the kayak on one side.

Sweep Stroke
(Pivoting
Turn)

To make a pivoting turn, the bow and stern paddlers will sweep in opposite directions on opposite sides. For example the bow paddler will sweep in a forward direction on the left side, while the stern paddler sweeps in reverse on the right side. This will cause the kayak to rotate in place clockwise from a top view.

Try this together using opposite forward and reverse strokes and opposite right and left sides. You will have no momentum while doing this maneuver and will have to start the kayak from a dead stop once you are pointed in the direction that you wish to go.

Try all these turning techniques in a practice session experimenting with all the different combinations. Don't be discouraged if you whack your paddles or have difficulty in turning the way you intended. You will feel uncoordinated and dyslexic for a while until you have got the hang of it. When you turn your Tandem kayak you need to work together. Always communicate your intentions to each other.

Maintaining Stability

Bracing

When you experience rough water or other situations that cause your kayak to tip, you will need to prevent a capsize by using your paddle to brace. You can push down, with your paddle, to stay up, much like you push back to go forward.

Bracing

In concert with this you must allow your hips to go loose and let the kayak rock while your upper body remains stable and directly over the centerline of the kayak.

To brace, reach out to one side with your paddle, with the blade held flat, and slap the surface of the water. The motion should be a quick shallow spanking, like a beaver's tail sounding an alarm. You will find that the water feels solid and firm under the blade for a moment.

You can not lean on your paddle like a cane because the blade will sink down, providing only temporary support. Do not let the paddle blade go deeply into the water. It will get stuck down there and prevent you from bracing quickly a second time if necessary.

To practice this rock your kayak from side to side, grip tightly with your knee straps if you have them, and slap the water on each side as you tip. Feel the support that the water gives for a moment and tip to the other side to brace again.

Do this repeatedly rocking back and forth while saving your

selves form a capsize each time by bracing. If you are using a feathered paddle, it will be necessary to rotate the shaft, like with the forward stroke, as you alternate from the left side to right side.

Do this, with your partner, bracing together on the same side each time. The stern paddler will need to follow the lead of the bow paddler. Start out by leaning the kayak only a small amount and then tipping more and more to find out how far you can go and still recover.

Keep rocking and bracing more and more untill you fall in. You will discover your limits and get a chance to practice reentry technique. By practicing in this way bracing will become an automatic response to tipping.

Resist the urge to grip the side of the kayak, this will only make the boat less stable. Keep your hands on the paddle shaft at all times. Only by bracing with your paddle can you recover from a near capsize.

Hula Hips

Your hips are the junction between the rocking kayak and the stable upper body. Let your hips go loose, like hula dancing, and as the boat tips your lower body will react to the movement of the kayak while your upper body remains strait up and down, directly over the centerline of the boat. Do not let yourself rock like a metronome.

To loosen up your hips and get a bit of practice, wiggle your hips to make the kayak rock, while keeping your body strait. Rocking your boat with only your hips should cause small waves to spread in rows from each side of the kayak. This is called "hip snapping" or "hula hips." Take advantage of waves and boat wakes to put this in action and combine with a brace as necessary.

The Draw Stroke

You can make your kayak move sideways by using the draw stroke. This can be used to pull along side a dock or other kayak. The technique is simple and can be performed in reverse if necessary (called a pry.)

Reach out together with your paddles to one side and pull your blades to the kayak like raking leaves. This will cause the kayak to move slowly sideways. As the paddle blade approaches the side of the boat, rotate the shaft so that the blade is ninety degrees to the side of the kayak.

Draw Stoke

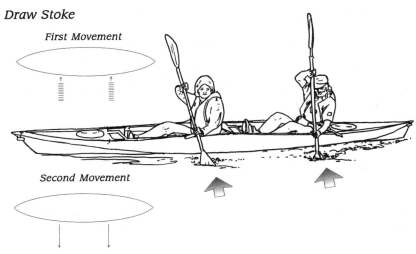

First Movement

Second Movement

Slice the blade, through the water, out away from the kayak back to where you started the stroke.

Repeat as necessary. If you do not slice the blade back out away from the kayak the paddle will drift under the kayak and pull you into the water. Practice this slowly and carefully at first.

Important Seamanship Skills 10

PADDLING IN WIND

Wind is the greatest challenge to the tandem kayaker. On days with strong winds, paddle only on protected waters. On better days plan your trips with the prevailing wind directions in mind.

If you plan a trip where you start and end in the same place, paddle against the wind first, then return with the wind at your back. This way you will have the wind helping you when you are the most tired. If planning a trip with a different put in and take out, then plan to go in the direction that has the wind at your back.

Use caution while paddling on a coast with an **offshore** (away from land) wind. Do not paddle so far offshore that paddling back to shore will be too difficult. Use caution while paddling with an **onshore** (toward the land) wind. Paddle far enough offshore so that you will not be pushed ashore. This can be very important on a rocky coast with breaking waves.

Always be aware of the wind direction and strength. Anticipate how the kayak will be pushed by the wind and adjust your heading and plans appropriately. Winds can change dramatically over the course of the day. Research local weather patterns and forecasts. Plan an emergency landing along your route and use it if necessary.

Strong winds can also blow an unloaded kayak off a beach and into water, causing your kayak to drift away. Tie your boat to a secure object above the high water mark if such conditions exist.

A paddle leash, or lifeline is recommend for windy days. If you capsize, the wind can blow your kayak away from you faster than you can swim. A leash or lifeline can prevent this from occurring.

TIDES

Tides are the movements of the ocean waters due to the gravitational forces of the moon. The water at the ocean's shoreline will rise and fall two times a day.

In some regions this is only a foot or two; in others it can be considerably more. Tides can cause strong currents where ocean waters ebb and flow through narrow channels, in and out of bays and inlets, and around points of land. These currents are best avoided.

Use a tide chart for your area to determine the best time of day to paddle. The knowledge of local, experienced paddlers will also be invaluable.

Beach areas will change with the tide. At low tide there may be expansive mudflats to cross. Sandbars and rocks can appear where they were not detected before. At high tides you may find your sandy landing is deep under water and a rocky shore is all that is left.

When your kayak is beached on shore, make sure that the tide will not come up and float your boat away on the current. It is recommended that you pull your kayak up past the high water mark and tie it off.

RIVERS

Paddling on flat-water rivers is not particularly difficult. White-water rivers, however, are very dangerous. ***Training from certified instructors is mandatory. It is not recommended for any one to paddle in white water with out this training.***

Flat-water rivers, without fast currents, obstacles, and water-falls, do not require extensive training. You should be aware of the current; it's rate of flow, and where it is taking you.

Know what lies ahead. Dams, waterfalls, rapids, and steep banks with no take out are the dangers to look for. Stop and scout the river ahead if necessary and be prepared to carry your kayak on the shore to avoid these hazards.

Some flat-water rivers flow slow enough to paddle up or down stream. Other rivers will allow only down stream paddling. Some rivers have both slow and fast moving sections. The water level of a river can also change. When your kayak is beached on shore, always pull it up past the high water mark and or tie it off to something.

PADDLING IN WAVES

Waves can easily capsize kayakers if they are unprepared. Avoid high surf. Small to medium waves can be quite fun, but they can also throw you off your kayak and sweep it away from you.

Paddling in waves is, however, excellent practice. Even if you do not intend to be a wave rider you may need to navigate through the surf zone from time to time. Practice in small easy surf and work your way up to more difficult conditions.

Stay clear of swimmers in the surf. Your kayak can run them

over and injury could result. If you do a lot of kayak surfing, you will want to wear helmets, particularly the bow rider who is susceptible to being whacked by the rear person's paddle.

When paddling out through waves, keep your kayak pointed straight at them, not sideways. Your kayak is more stable from bow to stern than it is from side to side. The larger the wave coming at you, the harder you must paddle to climb the face of the wave. If you are not paddling fast enough, the wave will push you back to shore, and possibly toss you. Once you have passed the surf zone the waves will not be as big.

When returning through the waves, your kayak will want to go sideways and roll like a log to the beach. To prevent this, you must steer your kayak. Keep your kayak pointed to shore. The stern paddler must rudder on the side that you wish to turn toward, while the bow paddler leans and braces on the same side. Both paddlers should grip the kayak with their knee straps.

If you steer too much on one side, your boat will go sideways. It is necessary to steer a little bit on one side and then a little bit on the other side, constantly counter steering until the ride is over.

Once the kayak is sideways, also called "broached," there is little you can do to correct it. You can prevent your boat from rolling over by both bracing your paddles on the wave face while leaning toward the wave. Keep your elbows low and close to your body to avoid shoulder injury. Hold on tight to the knee straps with your legs, and lean the hull of your kayak so the bottom will strike any obstacles in the surf zone.

Waves in the open sea and larger bodies of water can appear ominous but they are nothing to be frightened of. Maintain your stability by keeping your hips loose and being prepared to brace as necessary.

DEALING WITH CURRENTS AND WIND

You may find yourself paddling across a tidal flow, swift moving river or strong cross wind. In this case you will need to ferry across the current or wind by pointing your kayak upstream, or upwind and slightly toward your destination.

This will allow you to paddle against the current or wind while at the same time reach your destination with out being swept down stream, or down wind. The stronger the wind or current the more you must angle against it.

Transporting Your Tandem 11

Two person kayaks are by nature heavy boats. In theory you will have a paddling partner who can help you put your tandem on the car. This will divide the weight of the kayak by two, usually making it weigh less than most solo kayaks.

There are many people who will not have the luxury of a strong able-bodied partner. They may be solo paddlers with a tandem kayak, an adult with small children, or a captain with a reluctant crew. A good roof rack and a bit of know how can make it easy to load your kayak on your car.

You do not have to have a big, long, and tall car to carry a kayak. The best cars for kayaks are sedans and wagons. Their lower height is preferable because you do not have to lift the kayak very high. Vans, SUVs and pick up trucks are harder to load, but can do the job.

Placing your kayak inside a van, or in the bed of a pick up will not work well. More than half the boat will stick out the back and want to sag down and drag on the road. Trailers are usually unnecessary unless you are carrying many kayaks.

There are many types of racks for virtually all types of cars. Car-top carriers can be as simple as foam blocks and straps, or the rack that came with your car installed by the factory. You also have the option of putting a high quality, multi sport roof rack on your car, van, or pick up truck.

Foam Racks

Foam blocks are very economical and can do a good job. The foam goes between the roof and the kayak. Place the blocks where the roof is strongest, near the windshield and rear window.

The bow and stern are tied to the front and back bumpers of your car and a strap goes over the top of the kayak and inside the open doors cinched up tightly, the doors close on the straps, and you are ready to go. The down

SOFT RACKS

TIE TO BUMPER

TIE INSIDE CAR

TIE TO BUMPER

side is that the blocks need to be free of sand and grit to protect your paint job.

Roof Racks

Factory installed roof racks by the car manufacture can be very good. Know what the weight limit is for your rack so you do not overload it. One tandem kayak is not too heavy, but if you add another kayak you may be close or over the limit.

Many roof rack accessories can be utilized with this style of rack, including rollers to make loading easy and contoured foam blocks to cradle the kayak.

Sedans, wagons and vans can have very good multi sport racks installed by a kayak shop. These racks can carry everything: kayaks, canoes, bikes, skis, luggage and more. Their advantages are many: larger load capacities, security fittings, sport specific adapters like bike carriers and kayak saddles.

They are engineered not to damage your car. You will not have to drill or screw into the roof of your car. Most notably in the benefits are the devices to assist in the loading of heavy boats. Visit a kayak rack dealer for more information.

The diversity of these racks makes instruction for their individual use too large to fit in this chapter. Make sure that you understand the directions and use your rack properly. The only down side is that this style of rack does not come cheap.

There are special racks for pick up trucks. They mount onto the sidewalls of the truck bed, like contractors pipe and lumber racks, which would work very well also. Most of these racks can fold down or be taken off and stored behind the seat.

If your truck has a top on the bed, you can put a multi sport rack on it. There are many mounting devices to allow this. Specialty accessories or foam saddle blocks can be used in combination with your pick up truck rack. Read the directions carefully to understand how to use the rack properly.

Car topping your kayak

Now that you have a rack on your car, it is time to put the kayak on top. Carry your kayak to the car using the handles bow and

stern. When you get to
the car, let go of the
handles and each of you
hold the kayak with both
hands, one person at the
bow and one at the stern.

Slowly lift the kayak
together to the rack, use
teamwork, and be
understanding of each
other's limitations. If one
of you can not lift to the
top, then the paddler
who can should set their
end on top of the rack and
assist the other paddler with the
other end.

Tie the kayak to the rack and vehicle
using roof rack straps. Do not use bungie
cords as they are not strong enough. You will
also need to tie the bow and stern to the front and back
bumpers of your car. Test your tie downs by grabbing your kayak
and shaking it forcefully. If the kayak and car move as one then the
tie down is good. If the kayak moves independantly of the car, then
you need to improve method.

If you are lifting your boat solo you will want to lift the kayak
from the center balance point. Installing some custom handgrips
can help you get a grip. Otherwise deck lines, backrest or
kneestraps might be a good hand hold.

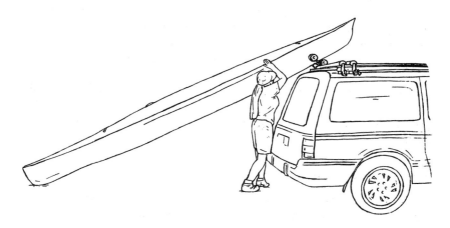

If the kayak is light and you are strong, then this may not be a problem. But if you find it difficult to load onto your car solo, you will want to look into accessories that help you get your boat on the car. Rollers and slippery saddles are good for wagons, vans and pick up truck racks. They will allow you to lift one end of the kayak, half the weight, to the rollers on the rear of the rack and then you can lift the other end while you roll the kayak forward into place.

If you have a sedan, then you may want an extension bar that pulls out over the side of the car, near the door area. Lift one end of the kayak onto the extended bar. Lift the other end and place the kayak in position on the rack. Slide the extension bar back into place out of the way. Finally tie the kayak to the rack and car.

You do not have to go out and buy a new car for your kayak, but take these thoughts in mind when deciding what car to use as your boat transporter. There is a way to carry every kayak with every car. Experiment and develop a strategy that works for you.

Using Wheels

There are times when you will transport your tandem kayak without the help of your car. You may want to consider the use of a boat cart to help you portage your kayak overland for moderate distances.

If you live within walking distance to the water you can skip loading your kayak onto the car and simply roll it to the beach. This can also apply to water access that is not handy to the parking area.

A boat cart can mount on the stern or in the middle of your kayak. If the wheels are mounted to the stern you will lift half of the weight of the kayak. If the wheels are mounted at the middle, you will balance the weight without any lifting at all.

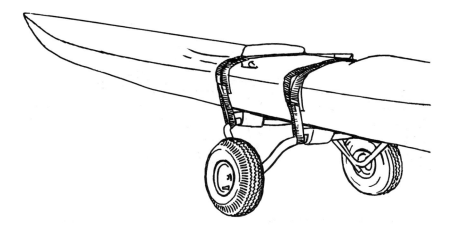

   Most boat carts strap onto the kayak and are easy to put on and
take off. Some carts fold, or take apart for storage. Depending on
your hatch size you may be able to put the wheels inside you hull. If
you do plan to store your wheels in the hatch of the kayak, shop for
a style and size that will allow for it.

Activities With Your Tandem 12

Once you have mastered the basic skills of tandem kayaking and experienced the satisfaction of navigating your kayak you will want to explore the variety of possibilities that the sport has to offer.

You and your crew can take your kayak on adventures that include: fishing, camping, diving, snorkeling, wave riding, wildlife watching, exercise, racing and more.

When fishing and wildlife watching, the person in the bow seat will have the greater advantage; while the stern person will be able to best control the kayak. This however does not mean that both can not participate. It is a good idea to keep a dry bag handy for your binoculars, field guides, and cameras.

Fishing

When fishing you will want to start with the basic tackle and rod, or handline. You will need a secure place to put your hooks, lures, and other necessities. A storage hatch or deck- mounted container will be necessary.

Rod holder

If you wish to troll (drag a line as you go) then a deck-mounted rod holder will allow you to deploy a pole while you paddle. You and your partner can troll at the same time if you point one rod holder to the left and the other to the right.

Tie your fishing pole to the kayak using a paddle leash or light line that will allow you freedom of movement. This will prevent loss of the pole if you capsize or if a large fish strikes.

You will need a way to secure your paddle while you are reeling in your catch. A paddle holder or some shock cords mounted on the deck is best.

It is possible to fish in one place by using a small anchor, or you may want to drift with the current while you cast your lines.

Diving and Snorkeling

Sit-on-tops have made diving and snorkeling from a kayak more convenient. You can easily slip overboard and explore the underwater world.

Store your mask, fins and snorkel in a mesh deck bag or storage hatch. Bring an anchor or towline so your boat won't drift away while you are under water. An anchor line should be much longer than the water is deep. More than three times the depth of the water. A towline should be held in the hand or have a quick release attachment in case of entanglement. Bring a bilge pump if you will be opening your hatches a lot. If you capsize with your hatch open you will need to bail.

You will want to fly a dive flag from your kayak so that other boaters know that there is a diver below. There are many ways to mount the flagpole to your kayak. The best is a rubber stopper with a hole in the center for the flagpole to fit in and then stuck into the scupper hole of your cockpit. A waterproof disposable camera can add to your fun.

Kayak diving is now a course offered at many scuba schools. If you are serious about scuba diving look into getting certified in kayak diving.

Camping With Your Tandem

Your tandem kayak can take you on a camping expedition. Find a wild coastline or river to explore and load your boat with your camping supplies.

You will need a tandem with cargo hatches. Position your gear evenly in the kayak, or with just a bit more weight in the rear. The heaviest loads like drinking water and food should be loaded low and in the center of the boat. Lighter stuff like clothing and bedding should be placed in the bow and stern. All your Gear should be stored in waterproof containers and dry bags. Plan and research your trip carefully. File a floatplan for your expedition, or any other trip for that matter, with a responsible person. Take note of who is on the trip (color of their kayak and PFD), where you will be going and when you plan to come home.

The things that you can do with your kayak are limited only by your imagination and common sense. Go out and explore, create new ways to use your boat and have fun.

The Right Tandem for You 13

There are now sit-on-top kayaks designed for virtually every possible use in mind so when purchasing one, it is important to ask yourself some questions.

Do I need a tandem or a solo kayak? If you know that you will be going solo most of the time then you will be better off with a one-man kayak. If you have a dedicated paddling partner, who will go with you most of the time, than by all means get a tandem kayak.

What will I use this kayak for? Think about your desires and goals. Are you looking for action or adventure, exercise or solitude? Will you be surfing, fishing, diving or touring and camping?

What design of kayak will help me reach these goals? You may find that you will outgrow your original goals. For this reason it is best to choose a sit-on-top that you can grow with.

Address these Questions with those who are helping you to make your purchasing decision. A salesperson at a kayak shop can be very helpful, but also seek a second opinion from a kayaking friend, an instructor, Internet forums or from magazines and books.

When you have narrowed it down to a few models, try them on the water in a safe environment, focusing on the test drive. Most shops will help you do this. Take your time and make your choice carefully.

Things to consider in choosing the best tandem for you are:

> ***Stability***
> ***Speed***
> ***Capacity***
> ***Performance in the specific conditions you will be in.***

Generally speaking:

> ***Longer will be faster***
> ***Shorter will be more maneuverable***
> ***Wider will be more stable***

Check to make sure that your gear will fit in the hatches or on the deck. Consider paddler(s) weight and that of your cargo and compare it to the kayak's capacity.

Most manufacturers supply specifications on each boat. Some

boats come with hatches, others can accommodate a later installation. Visualize yourself using the kayak you are thinking of, like a dress rehearsal.

The paddle choice is just as important as the kayak choice. It is not uncommon to think the performance of a kayak is poor, when the paddle is the problem. The more you intend to use the paddle or the greater you will depend on it, the higher the quality should be.

Choose your accessories with care. All areas require by law that a Life Jacket or PFD (Personal Floatation Device) be on you or within reach. Make sure it fits, does not restrict paddle movement, and is appropriate for your size. Special designs are available for women, children and even dogs.

When you are far from home and in rough conditions you will be depending on your gear. The best quality gear will then be essential. However, if you will be using your kayak just once in a while for short distances, then a lower quality will be sufficient.

Apply this evaluation to all your accessory purchases. Most shops should let you try the accessories that you are considering along with the kayaks that you are test paddling.

I wish you well in all your choices as you embark on this exciting, fulfilling sport. Happy paddling!

Kayak Safety  14

The water environment is quite inviting and fun but it can also be hostile to human life. Your life vest is your first line of defense. Always wear your PFD every time you paddle. Make it a habit and you will never be in trouble without it.

Arm yourself against danger by learning every thing you can about kayaking and the waters you will be paddling. Take a kayak lesson, join a club, learn from experienced paddlers, and study the sport through books, magazines, and websites. Practice what you have learned. Brush up on your skills, especially deep-water reentry. Challenge yourself with conditions that are just beyond your ability, but not way out of your league. You will gain experience by practicing, pushing your limits and experimenting. Develop a group of paddling partners of different experience levels to work with. You will be able to learn from each other and provide a safety net for each other as you challenge your skills.

Prepare yourself and your equipment. Study maps of areas that you wish to paddle. Make a plan for your adventure. Better yet, make a float plan and give it to your friend or neighbor. Seek out the advice of others who have paddled there before. Check your kayak carefully for damage like broken handles or strap eyes. Look for cracks or leeks. Make sure that you have your safety gear and that it is in good working order. You will rarely use safety gear but that is no excuse for leaving it at home or nor maintaining it. In the Appendix you will find a safety check list. Use it.

For long trips bring a repair kit. It should contain a few basic tools, spare parts, duct tape, some rope and string. A first aid kit is always good to have. Keep the kit in a dry bag or dry box. Check to make sure that it is dry inside before and after each trip.

If you paddle with a group, choose a lead kayaker that sets a pace that all can follow. The lead paddler should be experienced and well aware of the route. Choose a sweep paddler to bring up the rear. The sweep paddler should also have experience, carry extra safety gear and be prepared to assist any paddlers in the group that may need help. No one in the group should pass the lead kayaker and the sweep paddler must not let anyone fall behind him.

Good safety protocol not only will help prevent disaster, but will enhance your enjoyment of the sport and create group camaraderie.

Appendix

Several years ago
John Enomoto and I put together
The Safe Kayaking Check List.
It was following an incident where a kayak swamped
and was lost in remote, treacherous waters.
After hearing the survivors tell of the events,
we determined that practice in the use of the devices
on this list could have made a difference.
It has been revised many times with the help of Joseph
Hu and other members of our local kayak club,
Hui Wa'a Kaukahi.

Cut it out and use it.

Safe Kayaking Check List

This is a list of safety equipment
that all sit-on-top kayakers
should carry:

❑ PFD or "life vest" (coast guard approved)
❑ Drinking water in waterproof container
❑ Paddle leash &/or leg leash
❑ Bilge pump
❑ Knife
❑ Signal devices: whistle, signal mirror, flare, smoke, dyemarker, See Rescue, air horn
❑ Cell phone &/or radio in waterproof bag or "CellSafe"
❑ Spare paddle
❑ Proper clothing, aquatic foot gear & hat
❑ Flash light (waterproof) &/or strobe light for dusk or night
❑ Tow rope
❑ Helmet for surfing, rock gardens, whitewater rivers & seacaves
❑ Float bags
❑ Repair kit: duct tape, spare parts, tools, etc.
❑ Sea anchor
❑ Sun screen
❑ Sting aid
❑ First Aid kit

Carry as many of these devices as possible and
know how to use them.
PRACTICE
with them in a variety of weather conditions so you
can use this equipment no matter how bad it gets.
BE SAFE.
Always go with a buddy, and tell someone who cares where
you are going, what you are going to do and
when you will be back. Plan ahead and
BE PREPARED.

Glossary

Backrest: *an accessory to support the back*

Bilge pump: *a device for sucking water out of the boat*

Bilge water: *the water inside your kayak*

Bow: *the front of the boat*

Bowline: *a general-purpose rope attached to the bow*

Broach: *surfing sideways on a wave*

Bungie net: *lace work of shock cord to hold items*

Cargo deck: *a depression in the deck, often with straps*

Cockpit: *the depression in the boat where you sit*

Composite: *fiberglass, kevlar & carbonfiber material*

Deck bag: *a net bag secured to the deck for storage*

Deck line: *rope that runs along the deck for handholds*

Deck: *the top of the kayak*

Deckless: *without a deck to cover the hull*

Deep-water reentry: *getting on a kayak from deep water*

Dive flag: *a flag to indicate that a diver is under water*

Drain plug: *a cork in the deck to let out bilgewater*

Dry bag: *a waterproof sack*

Dye marker: *spreads on the water to make a signal*

Eskimo-roll: *method used to right an upside down kayak*

Feathered: *paddle blades at angles of up to 90 degrees*

Ferry: *to cut diagonally across a strong current*

Flare: *pyrotechnic device to create an illuminous signal*

Flatwater: *a body of water ie: lakes, oceans, calm rivers & ponds*

Float bags: *air bags to keep a swamped kayak afloat*

Float plan: *a detailed plan of your trip*

Footwells: *the place for feet*

Gunwale: *the outer edge of the cockpit*

Handles: *toggles on the bow and stern*

Hatch: *an access port into the interior of the kayak*

High stoke angle: *paddle held vertically for powerful strokes*

High water mark: *line between high water level & dry ground*

Hull: *the bottom of the kayak*

Kayak: *a paddle craft for one or two people*

Knee straps: *accessory for the legs to grip the kayak*

Leg leash: *a cord that attaches a kayak to the paddler*

Life jacket: *a flotation device worn for safety*

Life vest: *a flotation device worn for safety*

Lifeline: *a rope that attaches the paddler to the kayak*

Low stroke angle: *paddle held horizontally for easy strokes*

Moor: *to anchor your kayak*

Open-cockpit: *kayak with a self-bailing cockpit & sealed hull*

Paddle leash: *a cord to attach the paddle to the kayak*

Paddle: *a double bladed propulsion device*

Personal floatation device: *PFD, flotation device worn for safety*

PFD: *personal floatation device, life vest*

Portage: *to carry your kayak overland*

Power face: *concave side of paddle blade that pushes the water*

Put in: *the place where a paddling trip starts*

Rack straps: *tie downs to secure your kayak*

Rock garden: *a surf zone area with lots of rocks*

Rod holder: *a device mounted to the deck to hold a pole*

Roof rack: *two bars on top of a car to tie kayaks to*

Rudder: *a foot controlled device for steering*

Scupper: *a hole in the deck that drains into the sea*

Sea anchor: *a parachute for the water to prevent drift*

See rescue: *signal that can be seen from above*

Signal mirror: *a mirror for flashing a distress signal*

Sit-in-side: *traditional decked kayak; paddler sits in the hull*

Sit-on-top: *a kayak with a self-bailing cockpit and a sealed hull*

Skeg: *a fin on the bottom of the boat*

Smoke marker: *pyrotechnic to create a smoke signal*

Soft rack: *pads to put on your car roof for your kayak*

Spray skirt: *garment that attaches to deck & seals the cockpit*

Stern: *the back of the boat*

Sting aide: *reduces pain of stings from marine organisms*

Strap eye: *a small looped fastener on the deck for attachments*

Surf ski: *a long, skinny sit-on-top kayak for racing*

Surf zone: *an area where waves break along the shore forcefully*

Swamp: *to flood & sink partially into the water*

Take out: *the place where a paddling trip ends*

Tandem: *for two people, one behind the other*

Tankwell: *a recessed storage area on deck for cargo*

Tide chart: *shows the tides of each day for that region*

Touring: *long distance travel for exploration & fun*

Unswampable: *self-bailing, unable to sink or flood*

Wash-deck: *a kayak with a self-bailing cockpit and sealed hull*

Wave ski: *cross between a kayak and surfboard for wave riding*

Weight capacity: *weight the kayak can carry, people & cargo*

Whitewater: *river conditions like rapids, waterfalls & obstacles*

Index

A

anchor 66
apparel 28
avoid smacking your paddles 46

B

backrest 26
backstroke 48
bilge pump 66
bird watching 31
boat cart 62
bow 23
bowline 25
brace 51

C

camping 67
car 59
car-top carriers 59
children 32, 43
children's life vests 28
clashing paddles 47
clothing 28
cockpit 23
cold water 30
communicating 33
cross wind 57
currents 31, 57

D

deck 23
deep water reentry 41
dive flag 66
diving 66
dock 39
drain plug 23
draw stroke 52
dry bag 65, 67, 71
dry suit 30

E

emergency landing 55
extension bar 62

F

factory installed roof rack 60
feathered paddle 47
ferry 57
first aid kit 71
fishing 31, 65
fishing pole 65
fit your paddle 28
flat-water rivers 56
floatplan 67
foam blocks 59
footwell 23
forward stroke 45

G

getting back on your kayak from deep water 41
gunwale 23

H

helmets 57
high stroke angle 27
high surf 56
hull 23
hypothermia 30

I

inflatable kayaks 21

K

kayak saddles 60
knee straps 26, 57

L

Landing 38
launch 35
lead paddler 71
left handed 47
life vest 28, 71
lifeline 26, 55
low stroke angle 27

M

multi sport roof rack 59

O

open sea 57

P

paddle 27
paddle grip 45
paddle holder 65
paddle leash 26, 55
paddle size 28
paddling backwards 48
Personal Floatation Device 28
PFD 28, 71
play kayaks 19
portage 62
prevent a capsize 51
pry 52

R

racing 21
rack 59
racks for pick up trucks 60
re-enter 42
repair kit 71
reverse 48
rod holder 65
rollers 62
roof rack 60
roof rack accessories 60
rough water 51
rudder 25, 48
rudder stoke 49

S

safety gear 71
scupper holes 25
self-bailing 25
sideways 52
Sit-on-topKayaking.com 3
slow 48
snorkeling 66
solo 32
steering 31
stern 23
stop 48
storage hatches 25
strap eyes 23
straps 59
strokes 45
surf 56
surf ski 21
surf zone 35, 38, 56
sweep paddler 71
sweep stroke 49
synchronize your paddle strokes 46

T

tidal flow 57
tide chart 56
tides 55
touring 21
touring kayaks 19
troll 65

W

wave ski 19
waves 56
weight capacity 32
wet suits 30
wheels 62
white water rivers 21, 56
white water rivers
wind 31, 55, 57

Resources

GEO⬤DYSSEY
PUBLICATIONS

ORDER FORM

Please take my order for the following books:

"SIT-ON-TOP KAYAKING, A BEGINNER'S GUIDE"
by Tom Holtey   ISBN 0-9668655-0-2   ____ X 14.95= _____

"TANDEM SIT-ON-TOP KAYAKING"
by Tom Holtey   ISBN 0-9668655-1-0   ____ X 14.95= _____

                                        TOTAL BOOK PURCHASE $ _____

PLUS SHIPPING AND HANDLING
(1-4 Books = $4.00) (6-12 Books = $8.00)   +S & H $ _____

                                        TOTAL AMOUNT: $ _____

Make check or money order payable to GeoOdyssey Publications
For credit card orders please visit our website:
http://www.Sit-on-topKayaking.com

SEND MY ORDER TO: (Shipped via US Mail, allow 2 weeks)

_____

NAME

_____

ADDRESS

_____

CITY   STATE   ZIP CODE

_____

PHONE   E-MAIL

For large orders or additional information contact us at:

GeoOdyssey@aol.com

GeoOdyssey Publications
P.O. BOX 25441
Rochester, NY 14625

www.Sit-on-topKayaking.com
"A Paddling Place in Cyberspace for Open Cockpit Kayakers"

Learn more about Sit-on-top Kayaking basics...

This first book in the series covers solo kayaking skills, equipment and more!

Sit-on-topKayaking.com

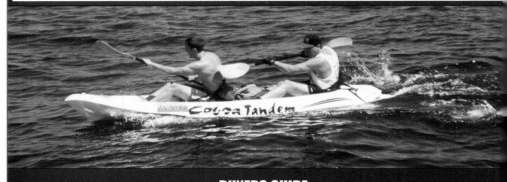

BUYERS GUIDE
A data base with the specifications of all known open-deck kayaks.

FREE CLASSIFIEDS
Classified ads to buy or sell sit-on-tops, equipment, & more.

ARTICLES
Learn from kayaking experts, as well as people just like you.

The on-line magazine & information exchange for open-cockpit kayakers.

FORUMS
Discuss a variety of topics with paddlers from around the world.

DIRECTORIES
Listings of kayak clubs, shops, outfitters, and schools.

BOOKS
A virtual book store featuring titles that apply to sit-on-top kayakers.

Aloha.

Meet Islander Kayaks — a brand new lineup of sit-on-tops that's destined to change the way you think about recreational paddling. Developed by the world's top boat designers and backed by the most rigorous R&D department in the paddling business, Islander Kayaks are all about simplicity and fun. Smart hull design allows them to track straighter, maneuver effortlessly (good news for beginners), and ride drier. Soft, rounded contours make getting in and out painless. And transporting is a breeze with the perfectly placed handles. So if you've been thinking about a sit-on-top — think about Islander. It's a good time. Guaranteed.

It Takes Two

...or in this case four!

COBRA KAYAK

Cobra Kayaks/Glenwa, Inc.
P.O. Box 3134,
Gardena, CA 90247

www.cobrakayaks.com
email: info@cobrakayaks.com

For a look at our line of kayaks, visit our web site or call us for a color catalog.

310.327.9216

Pictured with optional accessories

The Tandem

Easy to Paddle

Enjoy the outdoors, choose a Cobra Tandem for paddling with your family and friends. Cobra gives you a lightweight design (only 57 lbs.), a top deck that allows for up to 3 seats and up to 5 storage hatches...all at an excellent value!

Tough Materials

We use only **Super Linear Polyethylene**, a tough, long-lasting hull material that is extra stiff for a more efficient hull surface. Quickly and easily launches for a full day of fun.